$\mathcal{D}$ate

$\mathcal{T}$o my dear

with love from

Little Book of
Love Letters

Harold Shaw Publishers
Wheaton, Illinois

Compiled by Lil Copan

Edited by Elizabeth Cody Newenhuyse

Cover design by David LaPlaca

Editor's note: Many of these letters have been condensed and slightly adapted for the sake of brevity and clarity. Occasionally ellipses that indicate missing passages have been omitted. Any changes of meaning are unintentional.

03 02 01 00 99 98

10 9 8 7 6 5 4 3 2 1

To the One I Love:

Usually it's not polite to read other people's mail. But it's quite permissible in the case of these love letters—some hundreds of years old, some quite recent; some written by those of public renown, others from the pens of those celebrated only within their families. Through, in effect, peeking over others' shoulders, we can be inspired, touched, amused, and, together, strengthened in our own relationship by seeing how love works in the lives of others.

So open this bundle of ribbon-tied gifts—and know how much I love you!

Part 1

"You Fit into My Dreams"
New Love, Courtship, and Engagement

I made another song,
In likeness of my love:
And sang it all day long,
Around, beneath, above:
I told my secret out,
That none might be in doubt.

—*Robert Bridges*

Bernard Blakey and Josie Walker were married in 1929 after a courtship that spanned one year and many letters. Some of these letters were collected by their granddaughter Keri Pickett.

August 11, 1928

Dear Blakey,

I guess I should have been prepared for your marriage proposal, but I was not. Are you sure you really love me?

No one would enjoy a lovely Christian home more than I. However, a home can be neither lovely nor Christian without love and devotion on the part of both husband and wife. If I can come to the conclusion that I love you deeply enough, I shall be glad to enter into partnership with you.

Jo

Dearest JoJo,

When I stop to analyze why I love you, it isn't just your accomplishments and your need for me. It's just because you are you. Somehow you seem to fit into my dreams as though you belonged there.

Blakey

Letters between Woodrow Wilson and Edith Bolling Galt (later Galt Wilson). The First Lady, Wilson's second wife, played an active behind-the-scenes role in Wilson's administration, particularly after he became ill during his second term.

From Edith

Much as I enjoy your delicious love letters that would make any woman proud and happy, I believe I enjoy even more the ones in which you tell me (as you did this morning) of what you are working on—the things that fill your thoughts and demand your best effort, for then I feel I am *sharing* your work and being taken into partnership, as it were.

The White House
September 19, 1915

My noble, incomparable Edith,

I do not know how to express or analyze the conflicting emotions that have surged like a storm through my heart all night long. I only know that first and foremost in all my thoughts has been the glorious confirmation you gave me last night—without effort, unconsciously, as of course—of all I have ever thought of your mind and heart. You have the greatest soul, the noblest nature, the sweetest, most loving heart I have ever known, and my love, my reverence, my admiration for you, you have increased in one evening as I should have thought only a lifetime of intimate, loving association could have increased them. You are more wonderful and lovely in my eyes than you ever were before; and my pride and joy and gratitude that you should love me with such a perfect love are beyond all expression, except in some great poem which I cannot write.

Your own

Woodrow

From <u>The Adventures of Sally</u>, by P. G. Wodehouse: Sally is on the verge of a romantic relationship with Ginger. She writes to him about a visit with his relatives:

April 18

Dear Ginger,

Do you know Monk's Crofton? Probably you don't. I hope you haven't seen it, anyway, because I want to describe it at great length. I want to pour out my soul about it. Ginger, what has England ever done to deserve such paradises? There's a lovely stillness, and you can hear everything growing. And thrushes and blackbirds—oh, Ginger, it's heavenly!

But there's a catch. I can see now why you couldn't hit it off with the Family. Is it a habit of your family to collect in gangs, or have I just happened to stumble into an accidental Old Home Week?

I felt like a small lion in a den of Daniels. I know exactly now what you mean about the Family. They *look* at you! Of course, it's all right for me, because I am snowy white clear through, but I can just imagine what it must have been like for you with your permanently guilty conscience.

By the way, it's going to be a delicate business getting this letter through to you—rather like carrying the dispatches through the enemy's lines in a Civil War play. For it is no light matter, my lad, to be caught having correspondence with a human Jimpson weed like you. . . . Somebody mentioned you, and the most awful roasting party broke loose. I said feebly that I had met you and had found you part human, and there was an awful silence till they all started at the same time to show me where I was wrong. I tell you this in case you may imagine you're popular with the Family. You're not. . . .

Yours in the balance,

Sally.

Monk's Crofton,
Much Middleford,
Salop
April 20

Dear Ginger,–Leaving here to-day. In disgrace. Hard, cold looks from the family. Strained silences. Uncle Donald far from chummy. You can guess what has happened. I might have seen it coming. I can see now that it was in the air all along.

Yours moving in an orderly manner to the exit,

Sally.

Wartime correspondence between Mirren Barford and Lieutenant John "Jock" Lewes

From John

You and I, Mirren, are under test now; we have been since you first challenged me to know you and I challenged you to love. What is it we look for in each other for to love? It must be the heart's affections and imagination.

Darling, I love you and want you here because I love you and because together I think we could make a pretty good best of this bondage of flesh.

May God smile upon you and otherwise bless you for your man,

John

From Mirren

Oxford
January 19, 1942

Dearest love,

I went to see your parents to ask if they would accept me. They welcomed
me, and I didn't feel uneasy or shabby after all. The only thing is that after
the way they talked about you, so quietly, so sweetly and proudly, I wondered
all over again how I could possibly make a good life for you; are you still
willing to take the gamble?

John, how could I reach your mind across these leagues of sea and desert?
Somehow you've got to know, now, at once, how important it is that you
should send a cable [responding to mine]. Look, darling, you don't want me
to be bony and grey-haired, do you? Well, I've lost almost two pounds since
January 5th and if I don't hear from you pretty soon I shall be so ugly;
circles under my eyes and scraggy around the ribs, and you know you
wouldn't like that. So be good and tell me you love me very soon. You always
have my love and all I can do now is to ask the Almighty Powers to be
merciful and to keep you safe and free.

Yours ever,
Mirren

From Nathaniel Hawthorne to Sophia Peabody (later Sophia Hawthorne)

1 December [c.1839]

Dearest,—I wish I had the gift of making rhymes, for methinks there is poetry in my head and heart since I have been in love with you. You are a Poem. Of what sor then? Epic? Mercy on me, no! A sonnet? No; for that is too labored and artificial. You are a sort of sweet, simple, gay pathetic ballad, which Nature is singing, sometimes with tears, sometimes with smiles, and sometimes with intermingled smiles and tears.

From Bessie Huntting, a young teacher, to her fiance

Sept 26-7, 1858

Monday night 11 o'clock. I wrote you a long letter, *kind friend* at yesterdays twilight hour, for my thoughts rested on the memories of the Sabbath previous, but I laid it aside to join the loved circle [with] Sister Mary . . playing & singing those good old hymns. It never seems like the Sabbath, unles we have sacred music after tea. My dear father loved it so—and I know you love it, and join us in its rich notes of praise. . . . I welcomed your pennings by *to-day's* mail—the *outgushings* of *your thoughts* which *time* will sober, into deeper realities. . . .

It was 11 o'clock before our friends left and then I began this long epistle! may you not tire of it! but reply to it soon, and now I must say Good-night wishing you every blessing—prosperity in your daily cares and toils—"blessings in your basket and in your store," but do not forget to take care of *yourself.* Know thyself, fully & truly—and while I pray for thee, think kindly of your true friend.

Bessie H

From Elizabeth Barrett to Robert Browning

January 10, 1846

Do you know, when you have told me to think of you, I have been feeling ashamed of thinking of you so much, of thinking of only you—which is too much, perhaps. Shall I tell you? It seems to me, to myself, that no man was ever before to any woman what you are to me—the fullness must be in proportion, you know, to the vacancy. Was ever anyone taken suddenly from a lampless dungeon and placed upon the pinnacle of a mountain without the head turning round and the heart turning faint, as mine do? And you love me more, you say?—Shall I thank you or God? Both, and there is no possible return from me to either of you! I thank you as the unworthy may . . . and as we all thank God.

Have so much faith in me, my only beloved, as to use me simply for your own advantage and happiness and to your own ends, without a thought of any others. May God bless you!

Yours,

B. A.

From Hamlet, the Prince of Denmark, to Ophelia

To the Celestiall, and my Soules Idoll, the most beautified Ophelia.

Doubt thou, the Starres are fire,

Doubt, that the Sunne doth move:

Doubt Truth to be a Lier,

But never Doubt, I love.

From Dorothy L. Sayers's <u>Busman's Honeymoon</u>: *three letters responding to the news of Lord Peter Wimsey's wedding to Harriet Vane*

Mrs. Chipperley James To Hon. Mrs. Trumpe-harte

Well, dear, prepare for a shock! Peter Wimsey is married—yes, actually married—to that extraordinary young woman who lived with a Bolshevist or a musician or something, and murdered him, or something—I forget exactly, it was all ages ago, and such odd things happen every day, don't they?

Mrs. Dalilah Snype To Miss Amaranth Sylvester-quicke

Of course, *the* sensation is the Wimsey-Vane marriage. It must be a sort of sociological experiment, I should think. . . .

Miss Letitia Martin, Dean of Shrewsbury College, Oxford, To Miss Joan Edwards, Lecturer and Tutor in Science in the Same Foundation

Dear Teddy,

There was something rather splendid about the way [Lord Peter and Harriet] claimed one another, as though nothing and nobody else mattered or even existed.

The reception at the Dowager's was great fun—and for once, at a wedding, one got enough to eat!

Well—that was that; and I do hope they'll be most frightfully happy. Miss de Vine thinks there is too much intelligence on both sides—but I tell her not to be such a confirmed pessimist. I know heaps of couples who are both as stupid as owls and not happy at all—so it doesn't really follow, one way or the other, does it?

Yours ever

Letitia Martin

From Peter Marshall to his fiancée, Catherine

Dearest Catherine,

How last week dragged on leaden feet while I was waiting to hear from you. I really did not expect to hear until Friday afternoon or Saturday morning, but when no letter or card had arrived on Saturday morning, I explored all the torments of the lovelorn. I thought all kinds of things! I suffered agonies of secret pain. You see, I was waiting for the first expression, the first reassurance.

You will never know with what transports of joy I received your precious letter sent special delivery. It came about 10:30 last night, as I was working on my evening sermon. I read it with a bursting heart. I could have wept, and did—a little—and I thanked the Lord right then and there for giving me such happiness and such a wonderful sweetheart. Never in my life have I known such happiness and joy and peace. I cannot help thinking of the words of the hymn: "Peace, peace, the wonderful gift of God's love." Everything is turning out so much better than I could have planned it, because He is planning it. It was far better to get your wonderful letter at 10:30 last night than in the morning. It meant more to me then, for I had hoped all day and longed!

It was so hard leaving you on Tuesday night. I stood gazing after you a long time. . . . I can never be the same again. I am a different person now, praise the Lord, and you have made all the difference. My heart is in your keeping for ever and ever. I live from now on to serve Him and to make you happy. Life can hold nothing more satisfying or more glorious than this—the joy of building with you, a home that will be a temple of God, a haven and a sanctuary, a place of peace and love, of trust and joy.*

*About this letter and the beginning of their correspondence, Catherine wrote, "Thus began a correspondence rare in the annals of love-making. Certainly, there have been plenty of passionate love letters before. Literature has also preserved a few in which there runs a deeply spiritual note. There have been lovers sufficiently detached to write in a humorous vein. But I doubt if many series of letters, before or since, have more uniquely combined all three attributes."

We have promised each other—haven't we?—to be at least great friends. If you will only not change your mind! For there are no promises that are binding; such things cannot be ordered at will. It would be a fine thing, just the same, in which I hardly dare believe, to pass our lives near each other, hypnotized by our dreams: your patriotic dream, our humanitarian dream, and our scientific dream.

Of all those dreams the last is, I believe, the only legitimate one. I mean by that that we are powerless to change the social order and, even if we were not, we should not know what to do. . . . From the scientific point of view, on the contrary, we may hope to do something; the ground is solider here, and any discovery that we may make, however small, will remain acquired knowledge.

See how it works out: it is agreed that we shall be great friends, but if you leave France in a year it would be an altogether too Platonic friendship, that of two creatures who would never see each other again. Wouldn't it be better for you to stay with me? I know that this question angers you, and that you don't want to speak of it again—and then, too, I feel so thoroughly unworthy of you from every point of view.

Believe me your very devoted

Pierre Curie

Part 2

"If You Were Not Already My Husband I Should Certainly Fall in Love with You"

Companionship and Commitment

Oh, to be married to the one you do love, and love most tenderly! This is bliss beyond the power of words to express or imagination to conceive. There is no disappointment there. And every day as it shows more of the mind of your Beloved, when you have such a treasure as mine, makes you only more proud, more happy, more humbly thankful to the Giver of all good for this the best of all earthly gifts.

—*Hudson Taylor*

From Winston Churchill to his wife, Clementine

January 23, 1935

My darling Clemmie,

In your letter from Madras you wrote some words very dear to me, about my having enriched your life. I cannot tell you what pleasure this gave me, because I always feel so overwhelmingly in your debt, if there can be accounts in love. . . . What it has been to me to live all these years in your heart and companionship no phrases can convey. Time passes swiftly, but is it not joyous to see how great and growing is the treasure we have gathered together, amid the storms and stresses of so many eventful and to millions tragic and terrible years?

Your loving husband

From Zaduck Bamford to Frances Bamford, writing from the Australian gold fields

[8 October 1854]

Forest Creek Gold Fields

My ever dear wife and beloved children, it is with the greatest delight I sit me down to write these few lines hoping by the blessing of God they will find you all well as it leaves me at present thank God for it I have been on these gold fields but a few days yet and can scarcely speak of their richness but I hope to be able to save a few hundreds in three months And with what I have allready I hope to be able to see old England and them I love so dear I hope my ever dear dear and loving wife you have received the money I sent you 11£ on the 8th of August and 50£ on the 29th Sepr but a few days ago and as I stated in my last letter I shall bring the next myself O that will be a joyful meeting for us all and you see that I have not forgot you no all my thoughts are upon you and my little pretty children pray God bless you all is my ever fervent prayer of your dear husband I do work my dear wife very hard and am very saving it is for you and my dear little children to enjoy it with me when I come home you may be sure there is no enjoyment on these gold fields nothing but drunkenness and debauchery not fit for human witnesses diggers think nothink of spending 4 or 5 hundred pounds at a time and then set to work again for more and what I used to read to you at home on an evening is but triveling to what I witness I shall finish my work I am at on thursday next

One weeks work I took peicework and shall receive 15£ for it what think you of that and then I am off gold digging you would stare to see me with my jumper on and a six barrel revolver pistol in my belt by my side you would think I am some highwayman but every body is likewise armed. . . . every body can get plenty of money if they only take the trouble to work. . . . I hope my dear wife to be able to see you about our next birth days 21st and 23 of June then that will be a happy day. . . . adieu for a short time only my ever ever loving and affectionate wife and children

I am your affectionate and loving husband & father

Z. Bamford

From the forgetful G. K. Chesterton to his wife

[C. 1912—telegram]

Am in Market Marborough. Where ought I to be?

From Harriet E. Beecher to Miss Georgiana May, about Harriet's wedding and marriage to Calvin E. Stowe

January 6, 1836.

Well, my dear G., about half an hour more and your old friend, companion, schoolmate, sister, etc., will cease to be Hatty Beecher and change to nobody knows who. My dear, you are engaged, and pledged in a year or two to encounter a similar fate, and do you wish to know how you shall feel? Well, my dear, I have been dreading—and dreading the time, and lying awake all last week wondering, how I should live through this overwhelming crisis, and lo! it has come and I feel nothing at all.

The wedding is to be altogether domestic; nobody present but my own brothers and sisters, and my old colleague, Mary Dutton. . . .

Well, it is really a mercy to have this entire stupidity come over one at such a time. I should be crazy to feel as I did yesterday or indeed to feel anything at all. But I inwardly vowed that my last feelings and reflections on this subject should be yours, and as I have not got any, it is just as well to tell you that. Well, here comes Mr. S., so farewell, and for the last time I subscribe

Your own

H. E. B.

Three weeks have passed since writing the above, and my husband and self are now quietly seated by our own fireside, as domestic as any pair of tame fowl you ever saw; he writing to his mother, and I to you. . . .

And now, my dear, perhaps the wonder to you, as to me, is how this momentous crisis in the life of such a wisp of nerve as myself has been transacted so quietly. My dear, it is a wonder to myself. I am tranquil, quiet, and happy. I look only on the present, and leave the future with Him who has hitherto been so kind to me. "Take no thought for the morrow" is my motto, and my comfort is to rest on Him in whose house there are many mansions provided when these fleeting earthly ones pass away.

From Calvin E. Stowe to *Harriet*

[1842]

My dear,

You must be a literary woman. It is so written in the book of fate. Make all your calculations accordingly. Get a good stock of health and brush up your mind. Drop the E. out of your name. It only encumbers it and interferes with the flow and euphony. Write yourself fully and always Harriet Beecher Stowe, which is a name euphonious, flowing, and full of meaning. Then my word for it, your husband will lift up his head in the gate, and your children will rise up and call you blessed.

. . . And now, my dear wife, I want you to come home as quick as you can. The fact is I cannot live without you, and if we were not so prodigious poor I would come for you at once. There is no woman like you in this wide world. Who else has so much talent with so little self-conceit; so much reputation with so little affectation; so much literature with so little nonsense; so much enterprise with so little extravagance; so much tongue with so little scold; so much sweetness with so little softness; so much of so many things and so little of so many other things?

*after Harriet wrote to Calvin, telling him of her interest in writing

From Harriet to Calvin

[1842]

I was telling Belle yesterday that I did not know till I came away how much I was dependent upon you for information. There are a thousand favorite subjects on which I could talk with you better than with any one else. If you were not already my dearly loved husband I should certainly fall in love with you. . . .

From David Livingstone to his wife, Mary

Cape Town
5th May 1852

My dearest Mary,

How I miss you now, and the dear children! My heart yearns incessantly over you. How many thoughts of the past crowd into my mind! I feel as if I would treat you all much more tenderly and lovingly than ever. You have been a great blessing to me. You attended to my comfort in many many ways. May God bless you for all your kindnesses! I see no face now to be compared with that sunburnt one which has so often greeted me with its kind looks. Let us do our duty to our Saviour, and we shall meet again. I wish that time were now. You may read the letters over again which I wrote at Mabotsa, the sweet time you know. As I told you before, I tell you again, they are true, true; there is not a bit of hypocrisy in them. I never show all my feelings; but I can say truly, my dearest, that I loved you when I married you, and the longer I lived with you, I loved you the better. . . .

Let us do our duty to Christ, and He will bring us through the world with honour and usefulness. He is our refuge and high tower; let us trust in Him at all times, and in all circumstances. Love Him more and more, and diffuse His love among the children. Take them all round you, and kiss them for me. . . .

From a Chinese immigrant in Oregon to his wife

My Beloved Wife:

Yesterday I received another of your letters. I could not keep tears from running down my cheeks when thinking about the miserable and needy circumstances of our home, and thinking back to the time of our separation.

Because of our destitution I went out, trying to make a living. Who could know that the Fate is always opposite to man's design?

Because I could get no gold, I am detained in this secluded corner of a strange land. Furthermore, my beauty, you are implicated in an endless misfortune. I wish this paper would console you a little. That is all that I can do for now.

Walter Wangerin Jr., to his wife, Thanne: an open letter, from his book
As for Me and My House: Crafting Your Marriage to Last

Five years into our marriage I had returned to graduate school to complete residency for the doctorate. . . . I traveled to Oxford, Ohio, again; but because I had a family this time, a wife and children lost elsewhere in the bowels of America, I felt lost. This time I suffered a criminal homesickness.

I lived in a single rented room. I walked, between my room and my classes and the library. I walked through another autumn, and I remember that the trees burned with a cold, red fire. And I remember that all this color killed me. The very beauty of it made me want to cry.

And then . . . even before the winter came, you did.

One Saturday afternoon I stood on a bleak corner watching the traffic of High Street. . . . Then I saw our car. And your face so familiar behind the windshield, earnestly driving. And the kids, staring out at things, still not seeing me.

Oh, Thanne! How your coming loved me in an instant—the sight alone!

Any second now you'd see me. Thanne!

How long did it take to drive from Evansville to Oxford? Five hours? You drove five hours with three children at your ear so that we could spend a weekend together. And Mary was an infant, Matthew was a bouncing ball, Joseph a perpetual talking machine.

Then you noticed me, and your face smiled.

Why did you come? Because you loved me. By the very impracticality of the project, I knew you loved me.

Unreasonable! There was no pragmatic reason for us to be hugging in autumn jackets, in a sea of fallen leaves, in Oxford, in Ohio, on an insignificant Saturday. But we were.

Do you remember the moment?

From the Czarina to Czar Nicholas the Second

Tsarskoje Selo, Dec. 4th, 1916

My very precious one, Goodbye, sweet Lovy!

It's great pain to let you go—worse than ever after the hard times we have been living &
fighting through. But God who is all love & mercy has let the things take a change for
the better. Just a little more patience & deepest faith in the prayers & help of our
Friend—then all will go well. I am fully convinced that great & beautiful times are coming
for your reign & Russia. Only keep up your spirits, let no talks or letters pull you
down—let them pass by as something unclean & quickly to be forgotten. . . .

We cannot now be trampled upon. Firmness above all!

How will the lonely nights be? I cannot imagine it. The consolation to hold you tightly
clasped in my arms—it lulled the pain of soul & heart & I tried to put all my endless
love, prayers & faith & strength into my caresses. So inexpressibly dear you are to me,
husband of my heart. God bless you & my Baby treasure I cover you with kisses; when
sad, go to Baby's room & sit a bit quietly there with his nice people. Kiss the beloved
child & you will feel warmed & calm. All my love I pour out to you, Sun of my life.

Sleep well, heart & soul with you, my prayers around you. . . .

Ever your very, very,
Own

Two letters from George MacDonald to his wife, Louisa

Preston, Sunday Afternoon
23 October 1853

My dearest wife,

I have left the mamma and four children in the dining room and come here
to the study to write to you—which is more interesting than sitting with
another man's wife and children. . . .

How have you spent the day, dearest? It is a very good thing for us to be
parted sometimes. It makes us think more, both more truly about each other,
and less interruptedly about our God. . . . We may say to ourselves, one day
these souls of ours will blossom into the full sunshine when all that is
desireable in the commonness of daily love, and all we long for of wonder
and mystery and the look of Christmas time will be pined in one, and we
shall walk as in a wondrous dream yet with more sense of reality than our
most waking joy now gives us.

How is my Lily? and my sweet Blackbird. She laughs as the bluebird sings.
I hope dear love your cold is better. You are a dear good wife and your
husband loves you.

I am your own
George MacDonald

. . . Oh dearest, whatever you may feel about our homeless condition at present, I hope it has helped to teach your husband some things. Pray for him that he may not forget them but that he may be all God's and then let God give him what he will. We may wait a little for a home here, for all the universe is ours and all time and the very thought of God himself.

Again, dearest, your Husband.

Part 3

"One Day a Storm Tore Us Asunder"
Love in Wartime

Nothing has happened as we imagined it would except our children. We never thought we'd roam the world. We never thought our occupations and interests would cover such a range. We never thought that our thirty-third anniversary would find us deep in our second war and me again at the front. Well, darling, we've lived up to the most important part of the ceremony, "In sickness and in health, for richer for poorer, till death do you part."

—Theodore Roosevelt Jr, to his wife, Bunny

Camp Benjamin
April 1st, 1862

My own dear little wife,

. . .There is no thought more frequently uppermost in my heart than that which in imagination places us after this fratricidal war is over, beneath our "own vine & fig tree": cultivating the gifts which God has given us for usefulness & happiness and cozily brushing away all points of divergence between us. I scarcely think I do right in thus speaking in a way to draw to your eyes the pearly tears that, I am satisfied, are swimming on the brim of your heart continually; but it may be some compensation for my absence to know that thoughts of loved ones at home constitute the refrain of my waking songs & burden of my nightly dreams. At evening when the duties of the day are over, I sometimes feel oppressed with sympathy for you in your present delicate situation; and leaning against my tent pole I invoke the narcotic influences of my pipe to carry my mind far away into the ideal pleasures of dreamland. . . .

Write to me & tell me all about yourself and home. Love & Kisses—May God Almighty bless, comfort, & protect you is the prayer of

Your devoted husband
Will

From Kim Malthe-Braun (a Danish seaman, imprisoned and later shot by a Nazi firing squad), to his sweetheart

[1945]

My own little sweetheart: Today I was put on trial and condemned to death. What terrible news for a little girl only twenty years old! I obtained permission to write this farewell letter. And what words shall I write now? How shall they, my swan song, sound?

We sailed upon the wild sea, we met each other in the trustful way of playing children, and we loved each other. We still love each other and we shall continue to do so. But one day a storm tore us asunder; I struck a reef and went down, but you were washed up on another shore, and you will live on in a new world. You are not to forget me, I do not ask that: why should you forget something that is so beautiful? But you must not cling to it. You must live on as gay as ever and doubly happy, for life has given you on your path the most beautiful of all beautiful things. . . .

Lift up your head, you my heart's most precious core, lift up your head and look about you. The sea is still blue: the sea that I have loved so much, the sea that has enveloped both of us. Live on now for the two of us. . . . Remember, and I swear to you that it is true, that every sorrow turns into happiness—but very few people will in retrospect admit this to themselves. They wrap themselves in their sorrow, and habit leads them to believe that it continues to be sorrow, and they go on wrapping themselves in it. The truth is that after sorrow comes a maturation, and after maturation comes fruit. . . . I should like to breathe into you all the life that is in me, so that thereby it could perpetuate itself and as little as possible of it be lost. . . .

From Walter Savage to his wife, Meta

Naval Air Station, Cape May, N.J.
December 20, 1942

Dearest: You are wakened by the fire watch at 11:30 to be on watch by 12, and with considerable effort you climb down out of the sack to the deck and begin the wretched scramble in the dark to get into your clothes. You curse your fate then, and the crusty granules of sleep seem to have congealed forever upon your lids so that it seems they will never open again. . . .

Well, out into the night air, bundled and galoshed, the crystalline evening stretching vast upon the blue-seeming snow. . . . As the snow squeaks and complains under your feet, a shout rings out: "Halt! Who goes there?" and you reply "Aerology." "Advance and be recognized." You are identified and the sailor on the sea wall watch talks with you a moment trying to elicit some hope for a break in the temperature.

I am an inveterate city dweller, but I can love this wild, flat, windy and desolate coast as well, and my heart is out there with the boys in the convoys that pass nigh so that we can see the boats through the theodolite [telescope].

And so you take to examining yourself, assuring yourself that you must be here, as though you were wedded to it, and it is true, love brought you here, love of your wife, of your people, of life, freedom, and love of all the simple, oppressed peoples of the world.

All my love, Walter

Letters between Abigail Adams and John Adams

From Abigail

[31 March 1776]

I wish you would ever write me a Letter half as long as I write you; and tell me if you may where your Fleet are gone? What sort of Defence Virginia can make against our common Enemy? Whether it is so situated as to make an able Defence?

Do not you want to see Boston; I am fearfull of the small pox, or I should have been in before this time. I got Mr Crane to go to our House and see what state it was in. I find it has been occupied by one of the Doctors of a Regiment, very dirty, but no other damage has been done to it. The few things which were left in it are all gone. Cranch has the key which he never deliverd up. I have wrote to him for it and am determined to get it cleand as soon as possible and shut it up.

I feel very differently at the approach of spring to what I did a month ago. We knew not then whether we could plant or sow with safety, whether when we had toild we could reap the fruits of our own industery, whether we could rest in our own Cottages, or whether we should not be driven from the sea coasts to seek shelter in the wilderness, but now we feel as if we might sit under our own vine and eat the good of the land.

I feel a gaieti de Coar [French *coeur,* heart] to which before I was a stranger. I think the Sun looks brighter, the Birds sing more melodiously, and Nature puts on a more chearfull countenance. We feel a temporary peace, and the poor fugitives are returning to their deserted habitations.

I long to hear that you have declared an independency—and by the way in the new Code of Laws which I suppose it will be necessary for you to make I desire you would Remember the Ladies, and be more generous and favourable to them than your ancestors. Do not put such unlimited power into the hands of the Husbands. Remember all Men would be tyrants if they could. If perticuliar care and attention is not paid to the Laidies we are determined to foment a Rebelion, and will not hold ourselves bound by any Laws in which we have no voice, or Representation.

That your Sex are Naturally Tyrannical is a Truth so thoroughly established as to admit of no dispute, but such of you as wish to be happy willingly give up the harsh title of Master for the more tender and endearing one of Friend.

John to Abigail

[14 April 1776]

You justly complain of my short Letters, but the critical State of Things and the Multiplicity of Avocations must plead my Excuse. You ask where the Fleet is. The enclosed Papers will inform you. You ask what Sort of Defence Virginia can make. I believe they will make an able Defence. Their Militia and minute Men have been some time employed in training them selves, and they have Nine Battallions of regulars as they call them, maintained among them, under good Officers, at the Continental Expence. Their neighbouring Sister or rather Daughter Colony of North Carolina, which is a warlike Colony, and has several Battallions at the Continental Expence, as well as a pretty good Militia, are ready to assist them, and they are in very good Spirits, and seem determined to make a brave Resistance. The Gentry are very rich, and the common People very poor. This Inequality of Property, gives an Aristocratical Turn to all their Proceedings, and occasions a strong Aversion in their Patricians, to Common Sense. But the Spirit of these Barons, is coming down, and it must submit.

You have given me some Pleasure, by your Account of a certain House in Queen Street. I had burned it, long ago, in Imagination. It rises now to my View. . . .

Your Description of your own Gaiety de Coeur, charms me. Thanks be to God you have just Cause to rejoice—and may the bright Prospect be obscured by no Cloud.

As to Declarations of Independency, be patient. Read our Privateering Laws, and our Commercial Laws. What signifies a Word.

As to your extraordinary Code of Laws, I cannot but laugh. We have been told that our Struggle has loosened the bands of Government every where. That Children and Apprentices were disobedient; that schools and Colledges were grown turbulent. . . . But your Letter was the first Intimation that another Tribe more numerous and powerfull than all the rest were grown discontented.

Depend upon it, We know better than to repeal our Masculine systems. Altho they are in full Force, you know they are little more than Theory. We dare not exert our Power in its full Latitude. We are obliged to go fair, and softly, and in Practice you know We are the subjects. We have only the Name of Masters, and rather than give up this, which would compleatly subject Us to the Despotism of the Peticoat, I hope General Washington, and all our brave Heroes would fight. . . .

From General George E. Pickett to his fiancée, La Salle Corbell

In Camp, April 15, 1863

This morning I awakened from a beautiful dream, and while its glory still overshadows the waking and fills my soul with radiance I write to make an earnest request: entreating, praying, that you will grant it. You know, my sweetheart, we have no prophets in these days to tell us how near or how far is the end of this awful struggle. If the battle is not to the strong, then we may win; but when all our ports are closed and the world is against us, when for us a man killed is a man lost, while Grant may have twenty-five of every nation to replace one of his, it seems that the battle is to the strong. So often already has hope been dashed to the winds. . . .

Now, my Sallie, may angels guide my pen and help me to write—help me to voice this longing desire of my heart and to intercede for me with you for a speedy fulfillment of your promise to be my wife. As you know, it is imperative that I should remain at my post and absolutely impossible for me to come for you. So you will have to come to me. Will you, dear? Will you come? Can't your beautiful eyes see beyond the mist of my eagerness and anxiety that in the bewilderment of my worship—worshiping, as I do, one so divinely right, and feeling that my love is returned—how hard it is for me to ask you to overlook old-time customs, remembering only that you are to be a soldier's wife? A week, a day, an hour, as your husband, would engulf in its great joy all my past woes and ameliorate all future fears.

So, my precious one, don't delay; send me a line back by Jackerie saying you will come. Come at once, my own, into this valley of the shadow of uncertainty, and make certain the comfort that if I should fall I shall fall as your husband.

Your devoted,

Soldier

From Private Keith Winston, during the Second World War, to his wife

At sea (October)

My dearest Darling:

I received your letter, written after you were convinced I was going over, and your reactions were identical to mine. You know, dear, I never realized that my family would be the only thing on my mind when leaving. I knew it would be uppermost, but surely I felt I'd be thinking of the boat ride—would I be seasick—where in God's world were we headed—would I ever come back. And once on the boat I was sure I'd be constantly worrying about the crossing hazards—the subs and mines.

But strangely enough none of that seems to bother me—in fact I'm hardly concerned. The only thing I can think of now is that every day and every mile on this boat takes me farther and farther away from you and our boys.

There's absolutely nothing to do on ship. We sit on deck when and if we find the room—no comforts whatsoever. If I'm not talking with someone, I'm thinking of you and the children, and yearn and yearn and yearn, and as I realize the ship is taking me farther away from you, it becomes unbearable. . . .

From Sam Potasznik, a member of the Brussels underground who was sentenced for assassinating a Gestapo official, to his wife

Brussels
8 September 1943

My dear Doll,

These are the last words which I will write to you, since tomorrow morning, at dawn, I am to be shot. I am sad that I was unable to see either you or the children again before my death. But there is nothing that can be done about it. I must accept this. My dear Doll, my last moments are entirely devoted to you and the children. . . .

I implore you, . . . my beloved Doll, to forgive me for all the harm which I have caused you by leaving you in such a difficult situation. . . . I return . . . to [the upbringing of] our children, dear beloved; teach them to live a simple life without much useless noise, a life amid nature, and teach them to love beauty. Actually I have realized that one of my greatest faults was that I wanted everything at once. Work, studies and all the rest of it. . . .

When I review, in my memory, our life together, I find beautiful moments, but also bad ones. Anyway, I can assure you that I have always loved you from the depth of my heart. Maybe I did not always know how to reveal this to you, which I should have done. You know very well that this is a fault of my character. Please pardon me for this, now when the hour of my death is approaching, you, my beloved, and please think above all of the happy times we have spent together. . . .

Goodbye, my love, I kiss you tenderly for the last time,

Sam

From Maria von Wedemeyer to Dietrich Bonhoeffer, a German pastor who was imprisoned and eventually hanged for his part in a plot to kill Hitler

Altenburg, 13 January 194[4]

My very dear Dietrich,

Today is the first anniversary of our engagement. There's really no more to be said on the subject. All day long I've been thinking "One year, one year," and nothing else. It was a very long year. . . .

Nighttime

. . . I watched the clouds as I sat on my windowsill this evening. They drew nearer, merged with one another, and then dissolved again. It was as if all the unpredictability and inexorability of events were taking on shape, becoming perceptible and comprehensible.

I'm so wistful, Dietrich—wistful as can be. I so love to sit curled up on the windowsill, gazing at the sky. Then I have a little piece of it all to myself. And I send my dreams up into heaven and dream heaven down to me until I know exactly how various things stand, and how they'll one day be for us both: heaven on earth.

I've received two letters from you. How I'd like to look over your shoulder some time, while you're writing them. I often picture to myself how it must look when your hand travels across the paper, writing, and when you hold your head a little on one side and knit your brow because you're thinking. . . .

Thank you for your letters. I read them first thing every morning, and then I put them away in their envelopes during the day and look forward to being able to take them out again the next morning and reread them. That way, they're always new and dear to me. . . .

And now I'm going to see if the key is in the garden door and go outside for a while. Good night, sleep well, and remember that we'll soon be together and always remain so.

Yours,

Maria

From "Stonewall" Jackson to Mary Anna Jackson

June 4th. [1860] Little one, you wrote me that you wanted longer letters, and now just prepare yourself to have your wish gratified. You say that your husband never writes you any news. I suppose you meant military news, for I have written you a great deal about your *esposo* and how much he loves you. What do you want with military news? Don't you know that it is unmilitary and unlike an officer to write news respecting one's post? You wouldn't wish your husband to do an unofficer-like thing, would you? I have a nice green yard, and if you were only here, how much we could enjoy it together! But do not attempt to come, as before you could get here I might be ordered elsewhere. My chamber is on the second story, and the roses climb even to that height, and come into my window, so that I have to push them out, when I want to lower it. I wish you could see with me the beautiful roses in the yard and garden, and upon the wall of the house here; but my sweet, little sunny face is what I want to see most of all.

John C. Brock, Commissary Sergeant of the 43rd United States Colored Infantry

Since the last letter that I wrote to you, we have been engaged with the enemy. . . . On Wednesday evening we went to bed as usual. At two o'clock on Thursday morning a single horseman rode into camp, with a dispatch to our commander. Every man was ordered to strike his tent and get ready to march immediately. Soon afterwards long columns of troops commenced to march out past our camp. In about ten minutes every man was ready to march. But the order to move had not yet arrived; we lay there till broad daylight before we moved. Meanwhile the 2nd and 5th Corps continued to pass us in one continuous column. Many a man lay there with an anxious heart. They shook hands with each other, bidding each other farewell in case they should not meet again. One corporal from the State of Maine handed me a letter, together with his money and watch. "Write my wife," said he, "in case that anything should happen to me." He was only one out of the many that told me the same thing.

What a time for reflection! How many who are now well and hearty going out into the fray will never return again, and how many will returned bruised and mangled! Alas! alas! the desolations of war.

Part 4

"When My Last Breath Escapes Me, It Will Whisper Your Name"

A Love Rich in Years

The love of the old for each other has its poetry.
It is something sacred and full of riches.

—*Harriet Beecher Stowe*

Love Poem

That evening
The sky in the west flamed
Glory gold
As the sun sank.

Then the mountains in the east
Turned pink
And from the stream below,
The night breathed up,
Cold with the smell
Of water over rocks and moss.

I remember that perfume,
That light, that air
Against my skin.
But I knew even then,
That had you not been there,
Nothing would have been
As sharp or as sweet.

—Anne Keith, *Necessary Wind*

From a miner's wife (anonymous) in England, after her husband's death in a mining accident

[England, 1914]

. . . God took my man but I could never forget him. He was the best man that ever lived, at least I thought that, maybe it was just that I got the right kind of man. We had been married for 25 years and they were hard years at that, many a thing we both done without for the sake of the children. We had 11 and if I had him back I would live the same life over again. Just when we were beginning to stand on our feet I lost him. I can't get over it when I think of him how happy he was that morning going to work and telling me he would hurry home, but I have been waiting a long time now. At night when I am sitting and I hear clogs coming down the street I just sit and wait hoping they are coming to my door, then they go right on and my heart is broke.

Myrlie Evers-Williams, remembering her late husband, the assassinated civil rights leader Medgar Evers

I love roses, but Medgar could never afford to buy me a florist's bouquet. So he did something better. Every year he made a ritual of giving me bare-root roses to plant in our front yard, and eventually, three dozen rosebushes were the envy of our neighbors. Once in a while, Medgar would gather a bouquet, or perhaps just one rose, and hand it to me as he came through the door. It became an unspoken verse of the love between us.

One night he came in rather late, and I knew, from the set of his shoulders, that he was unusually tired. But when he handed me a single red rose, I knew something else as well. The rose symbolized love. And the color red, for us at least, meant fire. In his own subtle way, Medgar had set the mood for the evening. He placed the rose in a beautiful cut-glass vase he'd given me one Christmas and placed it on the table. The children were asleep. . . . I warmed his dinner and set the table with our cherished silver candle holders. Medgar lit the candles. I sat with him while he ate and talked about his day. Afterward, we moved to the sofa and Medgar reclined with his head in my lap. We stayed that way, in silence, for a while. . . .

From Jean Kerr to her friend, Madeleine L'Engle, recalling Madeleine's husband, Hugh Franklin

I remember well the first night we met you. The two of you seemed to tumble into our little house with happiness. Hugh in love was a different Hugh, boyish and buoyant. He was so enchanted with you. And we were so enchanted with both of you. And we talked and talked (I guess we always did do that). And the two of you slept (or did not sleep) on that tiny fold-down couch that wouldn't really fit one tall person.

I remember being startled when you told me that you used Johnson & Johnson's baby powder—because Hugh liked it. And when you both left the next day Walter and I were still in the afterglow of Hugh's happiness, your happiness, and our joy that Hugh had met and married such a marvelous girl THAT WE LIKED! How young we all were. . . .

Marietta Palmer Wetherill, a woman of the Southwest, reminiscing about her husband, Richard

He was one of those people that never got old. He was the same age when he died that he was when I married him. . . . Many times I felt much older than he because he was real boyish, you know. . . . He looked a hole right into ya when he looked at ya, very penetrating eyes. He didn't have time to put any fat on. He was too busy. . . . Even the years I was married to him I always called him Mr Wetherill. And still do.

[How we got together]: Father had been talking about Chaco Canyon. Mr. Wetherill had never been there, Father had never been there, and they wanted to see it so bad. So Richard said, "Well, I haven't got anything to do this winter much." He said, "How'd it be like for us to combine forces and take that trip down to Chaco? . . ."

We camped on the banks of the river and Mr. Wetherill said, "We won't try a crossing until the morning." And the next morning, quite early, he said, "Well, I'll try it." And I said, "I think I'll ride with you. I think I'd be afraid to ride my pony across all that water. It seems very wide to me." "Well, alright," he said. And so I got in the wagon with him and we started in and, well, just right now we were in deep water. . . . And I didn't say anything. I was scared. And we kept going on. We couldn't turn around because we were in deep water and the mules started to swim. . . . [When] we got out of the water, he said, "Were you frightened?" I says, "Why sure, I was scared to death." And he says, "Well, where do you put your fear?" I said, "I guess I swallowed it. I didn't say anything." "No," he says, "you didn't say a word." He says, "Will you marry me?"

Right then and there. And I said, "I don't know. I'll have to think about it." And he said, "Well," he said, "I think that it was meant that we should live our lives together and I'll do everything in the world to make you happy." And I said, "Well, I will, I'll marry you."

From John Calvin, about the death of his wife Idelette (née) de Bure, to Peter Viret

[1549]

Although the death of my wife has been bitterly painful to me, yet I restrain my grief as well as I can. . . . You know well enough how tender, or rather soft, my mind is. Had I not exercised a powerful self-control, therefore, I could not have borne up so long. And truly mine is no common grief. I have been bereaved of the best companion of my life, who, if any severe hardship had occurred, would have been my willing partner, not only in exile and poverty but even in death. As long as she lived she was the faithful helper of my ministry. From her I never felt even the slightest hindrance. During the whole course of her illness she was more anxious about her children than about herself. Since I was afraid that she might torment herself needlessly by repressing her worry, three days before her death I took occasion to mention that I would not neglect my duties [to her children].* She spoke up at once: "I have already committed them to God."

*When John Calvin married Idelette, she was a widow and mother of two

From Mark Twain to his wife, Olivia

Hartford, *Nov.* 27/85

We have reached another milestone,* my darling, & a very very remote one from the place whence we started; but we look back over a pleasant landscape—valleys that are still green, plains that still bear flowers, hills that still sleep in the soft light of that far morning of blessed memory. And here we have company on the journey—ah, such precious company, such inspiring, such lovely, & gracious company! & how they lighten the march! Our faces are toward the sunset, now, but these are with us, to hold our hands, & stay our feet, & while they abide, & our old love grows & never diminishes, our march shall still be through flowers & green fields, & the evening light as pleasant as that old soft morning glow yonder behind.

Your Husband

*her fortieth birthday

In these 34 years we have made many voyages together, Livy dear, and now we are making our last . . . You down below & lonely. I above with the crowd and lonely.

Twain's letter to his friend Thomas R. Lounsbury, after the death of Olivia

Lee, Mass., *July* 21/04

Dear Mr. Lounsbury: I know you are right. I know that my loss will never be made up to me in the slightest. The family's relation to her was peculiar & unusual, & could not exist toward another. Our love for her was the ordinary love, but added to it was a reverent & quite conscious worship. Perhaps it was nearly like a subject's feeling for his sovereign—a something which he does not have to reason out, or nurse, or study about, but which comes natural. It was an influence which proceeded from the grace, & purity, & sweetness, & simplicity, & charity, & magnanimity & dignity of her character. That & the frailty of her body, which made us nurse her, & tend her, & watch over her & hover about her with all ministries which might help out the poverty of her strength by riches drawn from our abundance. It was the attitude of more than one of her friends toward her, it was the common attitude of her servants toward her. Her servants stayed with her till death or marriage intervened: 12 years, 16, 19, 20, 22—that is a part of the record. And one is still with us who served her 23 years, & closed her eyes when death came, & prepared the body for burial. One that served her 20 years sent five dollars from his small savings to buy white roses for her coffin. Letters have come to me from shop-girl, postman, & all ranks in life, down to the humblest. And how moving is the eloquence of the untaught when it is the heart that is speaking! Our black George came, a stranger, to wash a set of windows, & stayed 18 years. Mrs. Clemens discharged him every now & then, but she was never able to get him to pack his satchel. He always explained that "You couldn't get along without me, Mrs. Clemens, & I ain't going to try to get along without you."

I thank you, Lounsbury, for remembering her.

Joe Twichell married us in Elmira 34 years ago, in her father's house; & on the spot where she stood as a happy young bride then, she lay in her coffin seven days ago, & over it Twichell spread his hands in benediction & farewell, & in a breaking voice commended her spirit to the peace of God.

Sincerely & gratefully

S. L. Clemens

July 14, 1861
Camp Clark, Washington

My very dear Sarah:

The indications are very strong that we shall move in a few days—perhaps tomorrow. Lest I should not be able to write again, I feel impelled to write a few lines that may fall under your eye when I shall be no more. . . .

I have no misgivings about, or lack of confidence in the cause in which I am engaged, and my courage does not halt or falter. I know how strongly American Civilization now leans on the triumph of the Government, and how great a debt we owe to those who went before us through the blood and sufferings of the Revolution. And I am willing—perfectly willing—to lay down all my joys in this life, to help maintain this Government, and to pay that debt.

Sarah my love for you is deathless, it seems to bind me with mighty cables that nothing but Omnipotence could break; and yet my love of Country comes over me like a strong wind and bears me unresistibly on with all these chains to the battle field.

The memories of the blissful moments I have spent with you come creeping over me, and I feel most gratified to God and to you that I have enjoyed them so long. And hard it is for me to give them up and burn to ashes the hopes of future years, when God willing, we might still have lived and loved together, and seen our sons grown up to honorable manhood, around us. I have, I know, but few and small claims upon Divine Providence, but something whispers to me—perhaps it is the wafted prayer of my little Edgar, that I should return to my loved ones unharmed. If I do not my dear Sarah, never forget how much I love you, and when my last breath escapes me on the battle field, it will whisper your name. Forgive my many faults, and the many pains I have caused you. How thoughtless and foolish I have often times been! How gladly would I wash out with my tears every little spot upon your happiness. . . .

But, O Sarah! If the dead can come back to this earth and flit unseen around those they loved, I shall always be near you; in the gladdest days and in the darkest nights . . . always, always, and if there be a soft breeze upon your cheek, it shall be my breath; as the cool air fans your throbbing temple, it shall be my spirit passing by. Sarah do not mourn me dead; think I am gone and wait for thee, for we shall meet again.

Sullivan Ballou was killed in the first Battle of Bull Run.

And in Closing . . .

And now, my strayed angel of the skies, my own, good night. May all blessings bless you, all sunshine shine for you, all angels guard you, all that is good take care of you and all heaven help me to be worthy of you.

Forever and ever

Your Soldier

—*from General George E. Pickett to his fiancée, La Salle Corbell*

Blessings be upon thee my best beloved—take care of thyself & continue to send me thy nice letters until thou comes to me thyself for evermore thy most affectionate Wife

M. Wordsworth

—*from Mary Wordsworth to William Wordsworth*

God bless you, darling, and keep you. We shall meet while we're young and stab old time in the back with a dagger from Joy Street, you see. Mirren, I love you. Bear with me while I say it again. I love you, and what I can of that love I send with the letter, but there's some that only your lips can receive from mine; that will not mix with this ink which is penned by your lover.

John

—*from Lieutenant Jock Lewes to Mirren Barford*

And now my darling Nellie, before I close let me invoke the choicest blessings of Providence upon you & our babe and His ever watchful care. Be cheerful, hopeful. Believe that you are ever present with me & lean upon me for comfort, consolation & support. Rely upon my constant affection; my unabated sympathy, my fixedness of purpose to bear all your burdens and brave all life's storms with you & for you alone; and may God Almighty in his abundant mercy throw the protecting aegis of his Providence around you & our babe & have you in his everlasting keeping until we are gathered together in his upper & better mansion not made with hands is the prayer of

Your devoted husband

Will

—*from William L. Nugent to his wife, Eleanor Smith Nugent*

Sources Cited

Love Letters from Cell 92: The Correspondence between Dietrich Bonhoeffer and Maria von Wedemeyer, edited by Ruth-Alice von Bismarck and Ulrich Kabitz, translated by Eberhard Bethge

John Calvin: A Sixteenth Century Portrait, William J. Bouwsma

My Dear Nellie: The Civil War Letters of William L. Nugent to Eleanor Smith Nugent, edited by William M. Cash and Lucy Somerville Howorth

Final Letters from the Victims of the Holocaust (from the Yad Vashem Archive), selected by Reven Dafni and Yehudit Kleiman

Kisses on Paper, edited by Jill Dawson

Myrlie Evers-Williams, "Remembering Medgar," *Essence,* February 1986

Love Letters: An Illustrated Anthology, Antonia Fraser

Love Letters, Antonia Fraser

The Heart of George MacDonald, edited by Rolland Hein

The Chinese American Family Album, Dorothy and Thomas Hoobler

Soldier of the South: General Pickett's War Letters to His Wife, edited by Arthur Crew Inman

Life and Letters of "Stonewall" Jackson, Mary Ann Jackson

Necessary Wind, Anne Keith

800 Years of Women's Letters, Olga Kenyon

The Oxford Book of Letters, edited by Frank Kermode and Anita Kermode

Letters from the Front, edited by John Laffin

Two-Part Invention: The Story of a Marriage, Madeleine L'Engle

A Book of War Letters, Harry E. Maule

A Man Called Peter, Catherine Marshall

Love in the 90s: B. B. & Jo: The Story of a Lifelong Love, A Granddaughter's Portrait, Keri Pickett

The Faber Book of Letters: Letters Written in the English Language, 1578–1939, edited by Felix Pryor

A Grand Army of Black Men: Letters from African-American Soldiers in the Union Army, 1861–1865, edited by Edwin S. Redkey

Busman's Honeymoon: A Love Story with Detective Interruptions, Dorothy L. Sayers

Edith and Woodrow: A Presidential Romance, Tom Shachtman

David Livingstone: Family Letters, 1841–1856, Volume II, 1849–1856, edited by I. Schapera

Hamlet, William Shakespeare

A Treasury of the World's Great Letters, M. Lincoln Schuster

Forever Yours: Letters of Love, selected by Ed Stackler

J. Hudson Taylor: A Man in Christ, Roger Steer

Life of Harriet Beecher Stowe Compiled from Her Letters and Journals, Charles Edward Stowe

Famous Love Letters: Messages of Intimacy and Passion, edited by Ronald Tamplin

Lines of Battle: Letters from American Servicemen, 1941–1945, edited by Annette Tapert

As for Me and My House: Crafting Your Marriage to Last, Walter Wangerin Jr.

The Civil War: An Illustrated History, by Geoffrey C. Ward with Ric Burns and Ken Burns

The Love Letters of Mark Twain, edited by Dixon Wechter

Joy Street: A Wartime Romance in Letters, Mirren Barford and Lieutenant Jock Lewes, edited by Michael T. Wise

The Adventures of Sally, P. G. Wodehouse

A Quilt of Words: Women's Diaries, Letters & Original Accounts of Life in the Southwest, 1860–1960, edited by Sharon Niedeman